YOUR KNOWLEDGE HAS VALUE

Nico Smit

Continuity Through Change?

The Erosion of Industrial Citizenship in Post-Apartheid South Africa

GRIN Verlag

Bibliografische Information der Deutschen Nationalbibliothek:

Die Deutsche Bibliothek verzeichnet diese Publikation in der Deutschen National-bibliografie; detaillierte bibliografische Daten sind im Internet über http://dnb.d-nb.de/ abrufbar.

Imprint:

Copyright © 2010 GRIN Verlag GmbH
Druck und Bindung: Books on Demand GmbH, Norderstedt Germany
ISBN: 978-3-656-43904-2

This book at GRIN:

http://www.grin.com/en/e-book/214621/continuity-through-change

GRIN - Your knowledge has value

Der GRIN Verlag publiziert seit 1998 wissenschaftliche Arbeiten von Studenten, Hochschullehrern und anderen Akademikern als eBook und gedrucktes Buch. Die Verlagswebsite www.grin.com ist die ideale Plattform zur Veröffentlichung von Hausarbeiten, Abschlussarbeiten, wissenschaftlichen Aufsätzen, Dissertationen und Fachbüchern.

Visit us on the internet:

http://www.grin.com/

http://www.facebook.com/grincom

http://www.twitter.com/grin_com

CONTINUITY THROUGH CHANGE?

THE EROSION OF INDUSTRIAL CITIZENSHIP IN POST-APARTHEID SOUTH AFRICA

UNIVERSITY OF CAPE TOWN

DEPARTMENT OF POLITICAL SCIENCE

THIRD WORLD POLITICS

NICOLAAS .A. SMIT

8/11/2010

CONTENTS

INTRODUCTION

Any discussion of industrial citizenship in South Africa is one which requires not only a focus on the current labour relations dispensation, but which tracks the development of labour relations in South Africa as it progressed along a winding path, beginning with the import of trade unionism from Britain in the latter stages of the nineteenth century.[1] From the outset industrial citizenship was not extended to all workers, with race providing the basis for inclusion and exclusion, and the dual labour relations system was formally crystallized in 1953.[2] Under the apartheid regime, labour relations created pattern of inclusion and exclusion on a racial basis which was swept away in 1979 with the state's acceptance and implementation of the recommendations made by the Wiehahn Commission.[3] South Africa's triple transition has been "accompanied by a process of corporate and workplace restructuring,"[4] engendering new patterns of inclusion and exclusion as South Africa has entered a globally integrated economy where exclusion is justified on the grounds of cost reduction and increasing competitiveness.[5]

This essay aims to make the argument that a large (and growing) portion of the South African workforce has roughly gone full circle in terms of industrial citizenship – where under apartheid they were denied labour rights and access to the industrial relations machinery, they are currently in a situation where the gains won throughout the liberation struggle and cemented in post-apartheid labour legislation are increasingly being eroded as they are shifted to a section of the workforce which finds itself beyond the scope of labour legislation. This paper is divided into four sections, the first providing a discussion of the dualistic labour relations system. The second section discusses the immediate legislative reforms effected in the wake of the 1973 Durban strikes, the establishment of the Wiehahn

---

[1] Robert A. Jones, "The emergence of Shop-floor Trade Union Power in South Africa," *Managerial and Decision Economics* 6 (1985): 160.
[2] Sonia Bendix, *Industrial Relations in South Africa*, 4th ed., (Lansdowne: Juta and Co, 2000), 52, 55; Martheanne Finnemore, *Introduction to Industrial Relations in South Africa*, 9th ed., (Durban: LexisNexis Butterworths, 2006), 25-26; Jones, 160; Francine de Clercq, "Apartheid and the Organised Labour Movement," *Review of African Political Economy* 14 (1979): 69.
[3] Finnemore, 29; Bendix, 74-6.
[4] Karl Von Holdt and Edward Webster, "Work Restructuring and the Crisis of Social Reproduction: A Southern Perspective," in *Beyond the Apartheid Workplace: Studies in Transition*, eds., Edward Webster and Karl Von Holdt (Scottsville: University of KwaZulu-Natal Press, 2005), 4.
[5] Von Holdt and Webster, 19.

Commission, its recommendations and the effect thereof on labour relations in South Africa. The third section focuses on the post-apartheid era, and the final section concludes

THE DUALISTIC LABOUR RELATIONS SYSTEM

The reach of the apartheid system was not confined to the socio-political realm, but extended to the industrial relations system and found itself reflected in, as well as shaping, the occupational and social structure of the workplace.[6] Where white and black workers initially "worked side by side" and shared mutual interests, cheaper black labour presented a threat to white job security and this, coupled with the emergence of Afrikaner nationalism slowly gave rise to widening "divisions in the sphere of labour relations."[7] Industrial unrest resulting from employer attempts at introducing "black labour into jobs reserved for white union members only" culminated in the 1922 Rand Rebellion, when violence broke out between white miners and the armed forces, resulting in a death toll exceeding 200.[8] Lacking formal legislative framework governing dispute-settling and negotiation between employers and their workers, the government responded to this incident by introducing the Industrial Conciliation Act (ICA) of 1924.[9] Representing the first comprehensive piece of "labour legislation to be introduced,"[10] the ICA was the first step towards a dualistic labour relations system as the omission of 'pass-bearing natives' from the definition of 'employee' effectively excluded this category of workers from the Act's provisions.[11] Based on the belief that "black employees were not sufficiently responsible to engage in collective bargaining,"[12] the ICA prevented black workers from joining registered trade unions, thus precluding them from the official dispute resolution and negotiation machinery,[13] a process whereby the state effectively

---

[6] Bendix, 55; Edward Webster, "Making a Living, Earning a Living: Work and Employment in Southern Africa," *International Political Science Review* 26 (2005): 56.
[7] Bendix, 55.
[8] Jones, 160.
[9] Jones, 160; Finnemore, 25.
[10] Bendix, 55.
[11] Bendix, 55; Finnemore, 26; Jones, 160.
[12] Bendix, 55.
[13] Jones, 160.

created one system of industrial relations for white, coloured and Indian workers, and another for black workers.[14]

The primary objective towards which the ICA was directed was the prevention of industrial unrest, a goal to be obtained via provision for "the machinery for collective bargaining and for conciliation in the event of dispute."[15] The Act and subsequent amendments to it provided for the creation of industrial councils and conciliation boards, and made any strike action that occurred in the absence of prior negotiation in either of these forums illegal, thus placing a criminal sanction on it.[16] The ICA also provided for mediation and arbitration, with the latter being statutory in essential services, and the Act further allowed for the voluntary establishment employer's associations and trade unions.[17] These organisations could register under the Act, "and together establish and register industrial councils,"[18] which then became the formally and legally recognized bargaining structures. Agreements reached at industrial councils became legally enforceable once/if gazetted.[19] The ICA provided a stable basis for the conduct of industrial relations, however, and as has been mentioned above, because black workers we excluded from the definition of 'employee', trade unions representing black workers were prohibited from registering under the Act.[20] The effect of excluding black trade unions from registering under the Act meant that they were also prohibited from joining industrial councils or applying for conciliation boards, and as a result, "could not...institute legal strike action."[21]

Despite the prohibition on joining registered trade unions, and the resultant exclusion from the industrial relations machinery, there was no provision preventing black workers from establishing and joining unregistered trade unions.[22] However, these unions faced a considerable challenge in that they were not recognised in the official dispute resolution and negotiation machinery, and the only means through which recognition could be gained was through direct second-tier negotiation with individual employers for substantive and

---

[14] de Clercq, 69; Johann Maree, "The Emergence, Struggles and Achievements of Black trade Unions in South Africa from 1973 to 1984," *Labour, Capital and Society* 18 (1985):286.
[15] Bendix, 61.
[16] Ibid.
[17] Ibid.
[18] Ibid.
[19] Ibid.
[20] Ibid.
[21] Ibid.
[22] Jones, 160.

procedural agreements, although these agreements were not criminally binding.[23] In passing the ICA, the state aimed to offset black workers from establishing and joining trade unions, and as a result, incorporated white, coloured and Indian trade unions into machinery that allowed for effective state control over them.[24] With regards to the unregistered black unions, the state, not at ease with their development, perceived them as sleeping giants with the potential to cause industrial instability and unrest as well as to call for political and social change.[25] As a result, the state reverted to a reliance on a heavy arsenal of repressive and coercive security legislation to outlaw organisations and band union leaders, and furthermore, the state employed its repressive machinery to avert marches, prevent meetings, picketing and demonstrations.[26] An increase in militancy of multiracial and non-racial unions, as well as those representing black workers continued in the face of heavy state repression and employer attempts to further erode their working conditions to the extent that it focused the state's attention on the issue of continuing unrest amongst black workers.[27] In response a number of government officials pointed to the wage board system – set up under the 1925 Wage Act – to be used to advance the interests and conditions of these unions' members, others called for the development of collective bargaining machinery for black workers.[28] A recommendation came from the Under Secretary of Labour as early as 1928 for the establishment of legitimate channels by which grievances can be voiced and the resolution of disputes by conciliatory means similar to the State approved methods for other workers.[29] The ICA was amended in 1930 to provide "for the extension of industrial council agreements to Blacks," and the amendment to the Act in 1937 "added to this provision allowing for representation of black employee interests on industrial councils by representatives of the Department of Labour."[30]

Black worker militancy continued unabated throughout the 1930s and 1940s, and when the Nationalist Party came to power late in the 1940s, Ben Schoeman, the new minister of labour, established the Botha Commission in 1949, with the objective of examining the existing labour legislation and industrial relations system in South Africa.[31] The mandate

---

[23] Ibid.
[24] de Clercq, 70; Maree, 286.
[25] Jones, 161.
[26] Ibid.
[27] Bendix, 65; de Clercq 71.
[28] Bendix, 61-2, 65.
[29] Ibid, 65.
[30] Ibid, 65.
[31] Bendix, 66; de Clercq, 72; Alex Lichtenstein, "Making Apartheid Work: African Trade Unions and the 1953 Native Labour (Settlement of Disputes) Act in South Africa," *Journal of African History* 46 (2005): 299.

afforded to the Commission by its terms of reference allowed it address what was seen as the "persistent problem of mixed trade unionism, as well as the pressing question of incorporating African workers into the ICA as 'employees'."[32] Recognising that union enfranchisement as well as parity participation in industrial relations and recognition under labour legislation might very well be perceived as precursor for wider socio-political enfranchisement, resulting in racial equality and ultimately putting white supremacy at risk, the Commission opposed this.[33] The Botha Commission did however recommend the establishment of separate bargaining structures for black unions and workers but "emphasised that recognition of black unions should be subject to stringent conditions and that strike action should be outlawed."[34] The government did not share the Commission's view regarding the encouragement of black trade unions, and accepted some, but not all – most notably, a total refusal of recognition to any kind form of black trade union – of the Commission's recommendations and passed the Bantu Labour (Settlement of Disputes) Act (BLA) in 1953, which later became known as the Black Labour Relations Regulation Act.[35]

Recognised as the "single piece of legislation that established industrial relations machinery for proletarianized Africans,"[36] the BLA formally crystallized the dualistic labour relations system. The primary aim of this Act was to counter and avert the development of black trade unions by providing for the establishment of an alternative means of consultation, namely in-plant workers' committees.[37] The BLA "established an elaborate, hierarchical and highly paternalistic structure of industrial legislation for Africans...that allowed for the Department of Labour to 'look after' their interests without any input from workers themselves."[38] The provisions of the Act provided not only for consultation via the workers' committees, but also for a "convoluted dispute-settling procedure which still out-lawed legal strike action."[39] Three years after the enactment of the BLA, the state passed the Industrial Conciliation Act of 1956 – which later became known as the Labour relations Act of 1956,[40] which became the new cornerstone "for labour legislation relating to collective bargaining." [41]It resulted in continued and increased polarisation as it "excluded all 'Bantu' (including

---

[32] Lichtenstein, 299.
[33] Bendix, 66; Lichtenstein, 299.
[34] Bendix, 66.
[35] Bendix, 66; de Clercq, 72.
[36] Lichtenstein, 296.
[37] Bendix, 66; de Clercq, 72; Jones, 161.
[38] Lichtenstein, 300.
[39] Jones, 161.
[40] Bendix, 67.
[41] Bendix, 67.

black African women)," placed a prohibition on continued registration of multiracial unions, unless by approval of the minister, and "placed restrictions on the registration of already mixed race unions and provided that such unions could not have mixed executives."[42] Furthermore, the ICA "introduced a system of job reservation whereby a particular occupation could be legally reserved for a certain race group."[43]

The abovementioned legislation served, more effectively than in any prior period, to entrench "racial division in the conduct of the labour relationship."[44] The discussion of these acts, and broadly their provisions, was aimed towards providing a description of the labour relations system prevalent in South Africa since the introduction of labour legislation in that country. That South Africa had a dualistic labour relations system formally sanctioned and legitimised by the state, is without question. Where one set of industrial relations machinery was developed and established for white, coloured and Indian workers, another set was developed for black workers, the only difference being that black workers and the trade unions representing these workers were excluded from the official industrial relations system.[45] Excluded from the formal definition of 'employee', and prohibited from registering under the legislation, black workers and the trade unions representing them were not only denied parity participation and representation,[46] but legislation creating an industrial relations system for them, was primarily aimed towards averting the development of black trade unions and ensure continued control and dominance over black labour.[47]

BIG RIPPLES IN A SMALL POND

The 1970s marked an end to the relative calm experienced in industrial relations during the preceding two decades as black workers were no longer willing to acquiesce to the secondary

---

[42] Ibid.
[43] Ibid.
[44] Ibid.
[45] Bendix, 55; de Clercq, 70; Jones, 160.
[46] Lichtenstein, 300.
[47] Jones, 161; Lichtenstein, 300.

status they had been afforded in industry.[48] Faced with dramatic increases in the prices of basic commodities such as fuel, clothing, food and transport, as inflation eroded the wages of African workers,[49] these affronts on the living conditions and standards of black workers "were at the root of numerous strikes, riots and lock-outs"[50] which occurred in the townships as well as at the point of production. This wave of unrest culminated in the eruption of massive strike action across Durban in 1973, in what has become known as the 1973 Durban strikes.[51] This strike, labelled as by far the biggest since World War II, involved more than 60 000 black workers, and rapidly spread from the Durban area to other centres, [52] brought the state to the realisation that "more fundamental change"[53] was necessary if it were to regain control over black labour. The state's reaction to the strike wave was immediate, passing the Black Labour Relations Regulation Act of 1973 which introduced a new system of plant-level liaison committees, providing an alternative to the workers' committees.[54] Because the 1973 strike wave exposed, in dramatic fashion, the shortcomings of the existing industrial relations machinery and labour legislation for black workers, the primary objective of the liaison committees was the improvement of communication between black workers and their employers.[55] Consisting of representatives of employees and employers, elected on the basis on parity, the liaison committees "could consult on any matter of mutual interest,"[56] however, once established, these committees often confined themselves to concerns relating to personal hygiene or other trivial issues.[57] The state nevertheless perceived these committees as a universal remedy "for all the problems that had developed, and obviously favoured them over workers' committees."[58]

Furthermore, the Black Labour Relations Regulation Act of 1973 extended a limited right to strike to black workers, and did so by establishing a dispute-settlement machinery "similar to that provided for in the Industrial Conciliation Act."[59] In addition to the expansion of the plant-level committee system and the limited right to strike, in 1974 the Voster

---

[48] Bendix, 72.
[49] de Clercq, 73; Steven Friedman, Building *Tomorrow Today: African Workers in Trade Unions 1974-1984* (Johannesburg: Ravan Press, 1987), 46; Finnemore, 28.
[50] de Clercq, 73.
[51] Bendix, 72; de Clercq, 73; Friedman, 46.
[52] Bendix, 72; de Clercq, 73; Finnemore, 28.
[53] Johann Maree and Debbie Budlender, "Overview: State Policy and Labour Legislation," in *The Independent Trade Unions 1974-1984*, edited by Johann Maree (Johannesburg: Ravan Press, 1987), 118.
[54] Bendix, 73; de Clercq, 73; Finnemore, 28-9.
[55] Bendix, 73; Finnemore, 28.
[56] Bendix, 73.
[57] Ibid.
[58] Ibid.
[59] Ibid, 74.

administration did away with the Masters and Servants Act, and allowed black workers limited participation in "Wage Board proceedings through the formal industrial conciliation process, *providing* issues designated by the Labour Department as 'affecting the African workers'."[60] However, by 1976 it had become apparent that the provisions of the 1973 Black Labour Relations Regulation Act had not provided an adequate solution to the "problem of black worker militancy." As a result, the state "appointed two commissions of inquiry into labour legislation,"[61] namely the Wiehahn and Riekert Commissions.[62] The Wiehahn Commission was tasked with investigating the state of labour legislation with the aim of making recommendations with regards to labour relations and the use of "labour for laws administered by the Departments of Labour and Mines,"[63] whereas the Riekert Commission was mandated to review the influx control system as well as other labour related concerns.[64] The appointment of these two commissions must be perceived as part of a wider state strategy designed to restore economic and political stability.[65] The Riekert Commission is beyond the scope and focus of this essay and thus no further attention will be devoted to it.

There were a number of significant forces driving the state's decision to appoint the commission of inquiry. Not only had the state come to the realisation that force and coercion no longer represented optimum measures of control, but since the Durban strikes of 1973, South Africa experienced and intense increase in black worker militancy which culminated in high levels of political and industrial conflict.[66] South Africa further experienced a shortage of skilled workers, a shortage which very well threatened economic growth, and which presented a significant concern to the apartheid regime as it required a strong and functioning economy to provide the resources needed to maintain capitalist and white domination.[67] Furthermore, increased international pressure over apartheid and racial domination, plus an increased threat of disinvestment and sanctions resulting in a disruption of trade gave credence to the notion that an improved image was badly needed.[68] This was the climate in which the Wiehahn Commission was established, and it appears very likely that the "Commission was specifically instructed to consider a method by which black trade unions

---

[60] Pearl Alice-Marsh, "Labour Reform and Security Repression in South Africa: Botha's Strategy for Stabilizing Racial Domination in the 1980s," *A Journal of Opinion* 12 (1982): 51.
[61] Maree and Budlender, 118; Bendix, 75; Marsh, 52; de Clercq, 74.
[62] Maree and Budlender, 118; Bendix, 75; Marsh, 52; de Clercq, 74.
[63] Maree and Budlender, 118.
[64] Bendix, 75; de Clercq, 74.
[65] de Clercq, 74.
[66] de Clercq, 75.
[67] Maree, 295.
[68] Bendix, 75.

could be controlled and incorporated into the industrial relations without creating too great a disruption." [69] this claim is supported when one considers the Wiehahn Commission's general strategy, namely, removal of the "sensitive focal points" of both external and internal opposition, "coerce black workers into more effective control, win over some strata of the black population, and reinforce the state-imposed separation between economic and political demands." [70]

The Commission recommended that black workers be allowed to establish and join registered unions and that union membership should be extended to workers of all races. [71] Furthermore, the Commission recommended that the legal reservation of specific occupations for whites be abolished and the establishment of an industrial court to "adjudicate on disputes of rights or interest and to create a body of case law," [72] as well as the interpretation of labour law. [73] Other major recommendations made by the Commission were: the removal of any and all race barriers to apprenticeships, [74] and "appointment of a National Manpower Commission to serve as an ongoing monitor and study group of the changing labour process." [75] The Wiehahn Commission argued that by extending registration to black trade unions, it would bring them under the same legislative control and regulation which the state exercised over other unions. [76] These controls placed on unions the obligation to have their accounts audited at regular intervals, to provide the industrial registrar with standard information regarding the union, and to draft its constitution in compliance with the specifications stipulated by the Industrial Conciliation Act. [77]

The state did not initially accept all the proposals made by the Wiehahn Commission, specifically rejecting the recommendation regarding the extension of trade union rights to all black workers as well as permitting the operation of multiracial unions. [78] The Government did however accept the Commission's major recommendations, not without caution, and in 1979 the Industrial Conciliation Act was amended. [79] The legislative reforms recommended

---

[69] Ibid.
[70] de Clercq, 75.
[71] Bendix, 75; Maree, 296; de Clercq, 75-6; Maree and Budlender, 119; Finnemore, 29.
[72] Finnemore, 29.
[73] Maree, 296; Maree and Budlender, 119.
[74] Bendix, 75; Finnemore, 29; Maree, 296.
[75] Finnemore, 29.
[76] Maree, 296.
[77] de Clercq, 76, Maree, 296; Maree and Budlender, 119.
[78] de Clercq, 75.
[79] Bendix, 77; de Clercq, 75; Maree, 296.

by the Wiehahn Commission "opened civil society,"[80] providing for the formal recognition of black trade unions within the official labour relations system for this first time in South African history, thus introducing a new era in South African industrial relations. Jones has termed the recommendations accepted as amounting to "a complete liberalization of the labour and trade union scene,"[81] including: (i) "The Abolition of racial job reservation;" (ii) "Allowing blacks into apprenticeship positions, and hence to practice as skilled artisans;" (iii) "The abolition of separate racial facilities in the workplace;" (iv) "The establishment of the Industrial Court to adjudicate on unfair labour practices;" and finally (v) "the establishment of the National Manpower Commission as a research, watchdog and advisory body."[82] The Act also lifted the prohibition on the registration of African trade unions, as well as the restriction regarding the establishment and joining of trade unions by black workers.[83] This change reached full implementation by 1981, and all reference to race was finally deleted from the ICA.[84]

The State's volte face regarding the concession of legal recognition to black trade unions as well as the extension of labour legislation to black workers should not be seen as morally or altruistically motivated. Faced with increasing industrial and political unrest internally as well as mounting international pressure, legislative reform was the optimal means by which the state could "co-opt African unions into the formal industrial relations system and...extend some form of state control over them,"[85] as well as present a picture of reform to the outside world. Nevertheless, industrial relations in South Africa stood transformed as the dualistic system was swept aside, and ultimately representing a transition which many have regarded as a precursor for the broader socio-political transition to come, and which the Botha Commission rightly foresaw.[86]

---

[80] Bendix, 77; Glen Adler and Eddie Webster, "Challenging Transition Theory: The Labour Movement, Radical Reform, and Transition to Democracy in South Africa," *Politics & Society* 23 (1995): 80.
[81] Jones, 162.
[82] Ibid.
[83] Maree, 296; Jones, 162.
[84] Jones, 162.
[85] Maree, 296.
[86] Bendix 66, Lichtenstein, 299.

THE POST-APARTHEID ERA

South Africa's transition to democracy was not only significant in political terms, but the transition can generally be referred to as a "triple transition,"[87] encompassing political, economic and social dimensions.[88] In terms of the political dimension, a move away from an overtly authoritarian state to a democracy has been witnessed; with regards to the economic, a shift away from a locally focused economy to one that has become globally integrated is seen, and finally, in terms of the social dimension, the transition encompasses wide scale redistribution of access to resources and power, skills and occupations.[89] Each of these transitions has had significant implications, but for the purposes here further attention will only be given to the political and economic. With regards to the political transition, for its purposes here, it established a platform for the creation of a vast range of social and democratic rights for workers. For instance, it created a platform for the establishment of legitimate institutions for consultation and negotiation between the state, employers and labour such as the National Economic Development and Labour Council (NEDLAC), as well as Bargaining Councils at industry level.[90] As mentioned above, the economic transition allowed the South African economy to become globally integrated, which has gone hand in hand with a process of workplace and corporate restructuring.[91]

Since the 1994 elections, the South African government has undertaken a systematic removal of apartheid legislation, and has replaced this with the "introduction of legislation designed to create equal opportunity throughout society."[92] With regards to the world of work, this has translated into the introduction of a new industrial relations regime, "made up of six core statutes – the National Economic Development and Labour Council (NEDLAC) Act of 1994, the Labour Relations Act of 1995 (LRA), the Basic Conditions of Employment

---

[87] Von Holdt and Webster, 4.
[88] Ibid.
[89] Von Holdt and Webster, 4; Richard Ballard, Adam Habib, Imraan Valodia and Elke Zuern, "Globalisation, Marginalisation and Contemporary Social Movements in South Africa," *African Affairs* 104 (2005): 615-634.
[90] Sakhela Buhlungu, "Comrades, Entrepreneurs and Career Unionists: Organisational Modernisation and New Cleavages Among COSATU Union Officials," accessed October 18, 2010, http://www.geog.psu.edu/courses/geog497labor/Readings/Buhlungu01_FESarticle.pdf
[91] Von Holdt and Webster, 4; Sakhela Buhlungu and Edward Webster, "Work Restructuring and the Future of Labour in South Africa," in *State of the Nation: South Africa 2005-2006*, edited by Sakhela Buhlungu, John Daniel, Roger Southall and Jessica Lutchman (Cape Town: HSRC Press, 2006), 248.
[92] Edward Webster and Rahmat Omar, "Work restructuring in Post-Apartheid South Africa," *Work and Occupations* 3 (2003): 4.

ACT of 1997 (BCEA), the Skills Development Act of 1998, the Employment Equity Act of 1998, and the Social Plan Act of 1998."[93] The LRA has entrenched and consolidated the workers' rights "won on the shop floor during the anti-apartheid struggle."[94] For the first time in South Africa's labour history all workers were brought under the scope of a single labour relations system.[95] The LRA has advanced collective bargaining by making provision for "organisational rights of unions in the workplace," in the process consolidating in law that which a number of unions had difficulty in achieving via private agreement: "access to employer premises, meeting rights, and union subscription facilities."[96] The new industrial relations regime has provided workers with an institutionalised voice, not only in the "workplace but also at the sectoral and national levels through industry-wide bargaining councils"[97] and NEDLAC. These institutional structures have afforded South African workers an unprecedented level of influence over social and economic policy formation.[98]

Thus, although the political transition has created a platform from which the organised labour movement has won considerable gains for workers, in terms of a floor of minimum standards which are solidified in legislation, the forces of globalization and the need to remain increasingly competitive in the global market has forced employers to search for ways and means by which to bypass labour legislation providing them with relative flexibility.[99] In this search for flexibility employers have discovered innovative means to undermine labour legislation as well as the minimum floor of rights for workers. This process has given rise to new, non-standard forms of work, such as casualisation, externalisation and informalisation.[100] To put this into context, workplace and corporate restructuring has simply re-organised patterns of exclusion and inclusion, which were so evident in the apartheid workplace, along new lines, brought about through the establishment of three clearly

---

[93] Ibid.
[94] Bridget Kenny and Edward Webster, "Eroding the Core: Flexibility and the Re-segmentation of the South Africa Labour Market," *Critical Sociology* 24 (1998): 217.
[95] Ibid.
[96] Ibid.
[97] Ibid.
[98] Ibid.
[99] Ibid, 221.
[100] Jan Theron, Employment is Not What it Used to Be: The Nature and Impact of Work Restructuring in South Africa," *Beyond the Apartheid Workplace: Studies in Transition*, eds., Edward Webster and Karl Von Holdt (Scottsville: University of KwaZulu-Natal Press, 2005), 301-2.

distinguishable zones, namely the core, non-core and periphery.[101] The latter two zones are comprised by workers engaged in non-standard forms of work.[102]

An understanding of the standard employment relationship (SER) is important in this context because South Africa's labour legislation is premised on the SER.[103] Although not a concept which enjoys legal status, the SER exemplifies a number of assumptions regarding employment, firstly, "that employment in an SER is assumed to be full-time employment,"[104] the implication being that an employee has one employer only. Furthermore, "the nature of reciprocal duties"[105] between employee and employer in law is closely tied to this understanding of employment. Secondly, the assumption is made that the employee carries out his/her work on the employer's premises, with the implication being that "there is a workplace that is controlled by the employer."[106] Finally, there is an assumption that employment is ongoing for an unspecified period of time, or permanent, and due to the fact that this expectation has significant legal implications, "the corollary is that there must be an actual contract of employment."[107] With regards to the three zones mentioned above, the SER is characteristic of work carried out by those employees found in the core zone, it being comprised by workers engaged in the formal sector.[108] Workers in this zone enjoy benefits; they have wages and have access to trade union and democratic worker rights.[109] With regards to the non-core zone, it is made up of workers engaged in externalised and casualised work, where employment relations are less secure; in some situations these workers may have part-time or temporary contracts with the core organization, and in other situations they have more precarious agreements with intermediaries such as informal factories, labour brokers or subcontractors.[110] Finally, turning to the periphery, this zone is comprised of people engaging in "informal-sector activities ranging from those that permit a degree of petty accumulation through subsistence activities to full employment,"[111] whereby they 'make a living as opposed to "earning a living."[112]

---

[101] Von Holdt and Webster, 5.
[102] Ibid.
[103] Theron, 311.
[104] Ibid, 296.
[105] Ibid, 296.
[106] Ibid, 296.
[107] Ibid, 296.
[108] Von Holdt and Webster, 5.
[109] Ibid.
[110] Ibid.
[111] Ibid.
[112] Webster, 61.

Turning now to the processes which have engendered the emergence of these three distinct zones, namely casualisation and externalisation and informalisation, the first refers to the process whereby use is increasingly made of part-time or temporary workers, "enabling management to vary hours of work,"[113] thus allowing them to achieve numerical or employment flexibility. Externalisation is central for our purposes here and refers to a process whereby the employment relationship is transferred to a nominal or third party employer instead of employing workers directly, thus rendering employment less stable, and reducing employee claims on the core employer.[114] Generally understood as outsourcing – a process whereby a core organization subcontracts a specific service to a satellite enterprise or contractor – it creates what is referred to as a triangular employment relationship between the employee, contractor and core business.[115] The employee is employed by the contractor, but works on the premises of the core organisation and is for all intents and purposes accountable to the core organisation.[116] This process enables employers to operate outside the legislative constraints developed which safeguard working conditions and to ensure a basic level of protection.[117] Finally, with regards to informalisation, the term refers to the process whereby the informal economy grows, encompassing activities ranging from those that allow a degree of small-scale accumulation through survivalist and subsistence activities to complete unemployment.[118]

Turning now to the effects which these processes, as well as the non-standard forms of work they have engendered, have had on workers and their rights, firstly, they have resulted in an erosion in the floor of minimum standards of workers.[119] Those engaged in non-standard forms of work are to a large degree not protected by labour legislation, and this lack of legislative protection has created a tier of workers increasingly vulnerable as they are unable to assert their worker's rights in the workplace, and have as a result become a tier of workers who are increasingly exploited by their employers.[120] Secondly, the processes of casualisation and externalisation have resulted in a re-emergence of patterns of inclusion and exclusion which have characterised the South African workplace significantly in the pre-1994

---

[113] Theron, 299.
[114] Von Holdt and Webster, 17; Marlea Clarke, "Ten Years of Labour Market Reform in South Africa: Real Gains for Workers?" *Canadian Journal of African Studies* 38 (2004): 568.
[115] Von Holdt and Webster, 17; Theron, 302.
[116] Von Holdt and Webster, 17; Theron, 302.
[117] Clarke, 568.
[118] Von Holdt and Webster, 17.
[119] Theron, 310-11.
[120] Von Holdt and Webster, 19; Theron, 311; Frank Horwitz, "Flexible Work Practices in South Africa: Economic, Labour Relations and Regulatory Considerations," *Industrial Relations Journal* 24 (1995): 263-4.

era. What one sees now, is that the processes of inclusion and exclusion are not ordered along racial lines, but rather along the creation of three distinct zones, namely, the core, non-core and periphery.[121] These three zones can easily be grouped further into 'haves' and 'have nots' in terms of stable employment relations, benefits, protection by worker and trade union rights, with those engaged in the core zone enjoying all of these and those in the non-core and periphery zones, experiencing the above to a lesser extent than the core, or not at all.[122]

Thirdly, the processes which underlie non-standard forms of work, and more specifically externalisation, have enforced a reconceptualisation of the workplace, and more notably who the employer is. In terms of the workplace, externalised employees do not work at the workplace of their employer, and many times their employer does not have a physical workplace.[123] These employees work at the workplace of the client organisation, who in terms of who the employer is, is not the employer of the externalised worker, but to whom the externalised worker is responsible for intents and purposes.[124] This is significant in that traditionally the workplace is the "site of labour organisation," and the employer's workplace is often the only place where "labour rights can meaningfully be exercised."[125] The process of externalisation stimulates the process of informalisation – meaning that it stimulates growth and expansion of the informal economy.[126] The informal economy, and its existence, in turn stimulates the two processes of externalisation and casualisation.[127] Externalisation, informalisation and casualisation "represent a trinity of interlocking processes," with externalisation exhibiting the profoundest consequences, and is due to the fact that "externalisation does not merely represent a dilution of the SER, but a shift away from the employment relationship altogether."[128] The significance thereof is, as mentioned above, that the system of labour legislation currently in South Africa is "premised on the existence of an employment relationship."[129] Furthermore, this "relationship has until recently been the *sine qua non* of trade union organisation [and]...similarly, it is a requirement for certain (but not all) forms of social protection."[130]

---

[121] Kenny and Webster, 243.
[122] Von Holdt and Webster, 5, 19, 29.
[123] Theron, 304.
[124] Ibid.
[125] Ibid.
[126] Ibid, 305.
[127] Ibid, 305.
[128] Ibid, 305.
[129] Ibid, 305.
[130] Ibid, 305.

South Africa has experienced an increasing trend in the use of non-standard forms of work, the result being that an increasing number of workers have become increasingly vulnerable, as those in the non-core and periphery zones are not protected by labour legislation as well as trade union rights.[131] Thus despite a degree of exclusion within and between the non-core and periphery zones, "it marks a process of reconstituting authoritarianism based on job insecurity," and in terms of externalisation, "on displacing the complexity of the industrial relations relationship in the stark simplicity of a commercial relationship."[132] Indeed, this calls to mind images of the "kind of labour flexibility experienced by black workers under apartheid prior to the growth of black trade unions, when they were subject to arbitrary and instant dismissal, as in a number of cases "the flexibility of migrant labour in the apartheid workplace regime is replaced by the flexibility of casual labour in the post-apartheid regime."[133] It is undoubtedly a case of continuity through change. The majority of workers in South Africa have gone through a process of exclusion-inclusion-exclusion in terms of industrial citizenship, as the drive for flexibility in an aim to remain globally competitive has, engendered an erosion of the worker rights, from which these workers were initially excluded, but over time won for themselves.

CONCLUSION

As mentioned at the outset, any discussion of industrial citizenship in South Africa requires a focus on the current system of industrial relations in that country, but also one which tracks the development of labour relations in South Africa from the inception of labour legislation. Starting out with discriminatory legislation which aimed to serve the interest of few at the expense of the majority, the labour relations system in South Africa from 1924 to 1979 is best described as a dualistic system, with one set of regulatory framework to govern white, coloured and Indian workers, and another set developed to govern black workers. This legislation allowed for the reproduction of socio-political apartheid relations in the

---

[131] Von Holdt and Webster, 5; Horwitz, 263-4.
[132] Von Holdt and Webster, 19.
[133] Ibid.

workplace, prohibiting parity recognition and participation in industrial relations, thus excluding the majority of the workforce from industrial citizenship. Widespread industrial and political unrest of the 1970s replaced the relative calm (in industrial terms) of the 1950s and 1960s; underpinning the state's realisation that coercion no longer represented a sufficient means to control the workforce, thus engendering a process of legislative reform which ultimately swept the dualistic system aside. South Africa's economic transition has however had one unintended and adverse consequence – the integration into a globally oriented economy has fostered the need to undertake a search for increasing flexibility,[134] and this has in the process given rise to the processes of externalisation, casualisation and informalisation. These processes have resulted in non-standard forms of work, form of work where those engaged in them are increasingly vulnerable as they are not protected by labour legislation, become increasingly vulnerable as their employment security is eroded and their working conditions deteriorate as they are increasingly exploited by employers.[135] Thus the phrase continuity through change effectively sums up the situation, although the country has thrown off the chains of authoritarianism, and moved towards a society that is fully inclusive, new means to and patterns of exclusion have emerged, and the segmentation that so distinctively described the apartheid workplace and industrial relations system, has once again become a significant characteristic of that in the post-apartheid era.

---

[134] Von Hodlt and Webster, 4.
[135] Horwitz, 264.

REFERENCES

Adler, Glen and Eddie Webster. "Challenging Transition Theory: The Labour Movement, Radical Reform, and Transition to Democracy in South Africa." *Politics and Society* 23 (1995): 75-106.

Ballard, Richard, Adam Habib, Imraan Valodia and Elke Zuern. "Globalization, Marginalization and Contemporary Social Movements in South Africa." *African Affairs* 104 (2005): 615-634.

Bendix, Sonia. *Industrial Relations in South Africa*, 4th ed. Lansdowne: Juta and Co, Ltd., 2000.

Buhlungu, Sakhela. "Comrades, Entrepreneurs and Career Unionists: Organisational Modernisation and New Cleavages Among COSATU Union Officials," accessed October 18, 2010. http://www.geog.psu.edu/courses/geog497labor/Readings/Buhlungu01_FESarticle.pdf

Buhlungu, Sakhela and Eddie Webster. "Work Restructuring and the Future of Labour in South Africa." In *State of the Nation: South Africa 2005-2006*, edited by Sakhela Buhlungu, John Daniel, Roger Southall and Jessica Lutchman. Cape Town: HSRC Press, 2006.

Clarke, Marlea. "Ten Years of Labour Market Reform in South Africa: Real Gains for Workers?" *Canadian Journal of African Studies* 38 (2004): 558-574.

de Clercq, Francine. "Apartheid and the Organised Labour Movement." *Review of African Political Economy* 14 (1979): 69-77.

Finnemore, Martheanne. Introduction to Labour Relations in South Afrca, 9th ed. Durban: LexisNexis Butterworths, 2006.

Horwitz, Frank. "Flexible Work Practices in South Africa: Economic, Labour Relations and Regulatory Considerations." *Industrial Relations Journal* 26 (1995): 257-279.

Jones, Robert A. "The Emergence of Shop-Floor Trade Union Power in South Africa." *Managerial and Decision Economics* 6 (1985): 160-166.

Kenny, Bridget and Edward Webster. "Eroding the Core: Flexibility and the Re-segmentation of the South African Labour Market." *Critical Sociology* 24 (1999): 216-243.

Lichtenstein, Alex. "Making Apartheid Work: African Trade Unions and the 1953 Labour (Settlement of Disputes) Act in South Africa." *Journal of African History* 46 (2005): 293-314.

Maree, Johann. "The Emergence, Struggles and Achievements of Black Trade Unions in South Africa from 1973-1984." *Labour, Capital and Society* 18 (1985): 278-303.

Maree, Johann and and Debbie Budlender, "Overview: State Policy and Labour Legislation," in *The Independent Trade Unions 1974-1984*, edited by Johann Maree. Johannesburg: Ravan Press, 1987.

Marsh, Pearl-Alice. "Labour Reform and Security Repression in South Africa: Botha's Strategy for Stabilizing Racial Domination in the 1980s." *A Journal of Opinion* 12 (1982): 49-55.

Theron, Jan. "Employment is Not What it Used to Be: The Nature and Impact of Work Restructuring in South Africa." In *Beyond the Apartheid Workplace: Studies in Transition*, edited by Edward Webster and Karl Von Holdt. Scottsville: University of KwaZulu-Natal Press, 2005.

Von Holdt, Karl and Edward Webster. "Work Restructuring and the Crisis of Social Reproduction: A Southern Perspective." In *Beyond the Apartheid Workplace: Studies in Transition*, edited by Edward Webster and Karl Von Holdt. Scottsville: University of KwaZulu-Natal Press, 2005.

Webster, Edward. "Making a Living, Earning a Living: Work and Employment in South Africa." *International Political Science Review* 26 (2005): 55-71.

Webster, Edward and Rahmat Omar. "Work restructuring in Post-Apartheid South Africa." *Work and Occupations* 3 (2003): 3-22.